SOBER
Revolution

Copyright © 2019 Teresa Rodden
All rights reserved
ISBN: 9781674438641

*Sober is making your days count,
not counting the days, you don't drink.*

DISCLAIMER: The information provided in this book is based on my life experiences. My intention is only to be helpful, not hurtful. This book and the content are not intended to diagnose, treat, or cure any medical condition, disease or issue, including alcoholism, substance use disorder, alcohol use disorder, or addiction.

Dedicated

to those that dare to

explore sober possibilities!

*Sober is making your days count,
not counting the days, you don't drink.*

Table of Contents

Introduction	6
Motive	11
Sober Intentions	13
Defining Sober	17
Sober References	21
Biblical Definition	24
Sober Scripture	27
Stages	34
Sober Thoughts	37
Sober Focused	40

SOBER
REVOLUTION

Alcoholism (SUD) or Coping	42
For the Record	44
No Diagnosis Necessary	47
Wholly Sober	50
Sober Possibilities	56
What's Right for You	59
Collaboration	61
Pink Cloud Coaching	64
Resources	69
About the Author	70

*Sober is making your days count,
not counting the days, you don't drink.*

INTRODUCTION

SOBER
REVOLUTION

Hello, my name is Teresa, and I walked out of the rooms of Alcoholics Anonymous over seventeen years ago and haven't had a drink in more than eighteen.

I have been abstinent all these years, but sober is another story.

Before submitting myself to outpatient treatment in January 2003, I had never thought about getting, living, being sober, recovering, addiction, or even alcoholism for myself.

In outpatient treatment, my education began.

There I learned that alcoholism and addiction are a disease, and there is no cure and that I will be managing my disease for the rest of my life. I learned that this is called recovery. I learned that the sober clock starts when you stop drinking and stops for reset the moment you take another drink.

And I learned the only criterion for being sober is not to drink, abstinence. That was my only choice.

*Sober is making your days count,
not counting the days, you don't drink.*

Desperate to change my life, I accepted all of it. During my first 58 days sober (abstinent), I didn't attend Alcoholics Anonymous. I think mostly because one of the outpatient counselors said she disagreed with the AA philosophy but never elaborated why.

On my 59th day, I attended my first AA meeting. Confident and proud, I shared something like, "I'm raising my sword to slay the dragon." Seriously, something like that. Long story short: I drank that night. I didn't get drunk or go on a drinking bender. I did proceed in beating the crap out of myself.

I cried myself to and through another AA meeting, convinced everything that they said was true. The disease made me drink. I couldn't help myself. I was damned with this monster inside of me for the rest of my life.

Through years of work, study, and research, I now know it wasn't "my disease" that made me drink. You can read all the details of that night in my book, Wholly Sober.

What matters for the intention of this content is I was, SOLD on everything they were saying. I proved it was all true. I was broken, diseased, and powerless.

I spent the next several months going to meetings, doing service work, and hanging close to my sponsor. And a little bit more. It was the little bit more that gave me the courage and audacity to do what it would take to break free and be wholly sober.

I made a brave and radical decision to leave the Twelve Step program and Alcoholics Anonymous.

Based on all that I had downloaded, I would most assuredly meet my drunken doom. But I couldn't fathom living my life believing there was a monster inside of me (the disease) waiting to take me down.

I concluded that if I had to spend the rest of my life talking about alcohol, I'd rather be drunk while doing so.

Yes, I was only in the program for a handful of months when I realized I had a new master--and it wasn't alcohol.

It was the "alcoholisms," the repetitive messaging and belief system that perpetuates an alcoholic identity.

All the things I must believe and adhere to do what? Abstain, commonly misidentified as sober.

> *Sober is making your days count,
> not counting the days, you don't drink.*

Since then, I have come to understand that abstinence and sober are not the same thing. It took me years to untie this knot—years of seeking, researching, studying, learning, and being willing to consider other possibilities.

I had intentionally detached from the identity of an alcoholic and got on with my life. But as I was learning about people I met in the rooms of AA going back out drinking, dying, and going to jail while they remained loyal members, I knew I had to do what I could to share what worked for me.

I hadn't identified as an alcoholic, being in recovery, or sober for years. It wasn't until I came across an article by Stanton Peele, Ph.D., questioning the disease theory and traditional recovery for over forty years, which piqued my curiosity about what sober truly meant.

Understanding the difference between abstinence and sobriety can be life-changing. It can be the missing link in your struggle and empower you to take charge of your relationship with alcohol or any other distraction that's in the way of you and the life you want to live.

MOTIVE

*Sober is making your days count,
not counting the days, you don't drink.*

The motivation of the Sober Revolution was to collect all my thoughts on this subject. I believe sober is completely undersold and misunderstood.

I implore you to open your mind and allow the content of this book to seep in and help you feel the bindings of deprivation loosen.

Sober is freedom.

Freedom to be curious, explore, and experience life with clarity and aim.

Freedom from labels, adapting to an identity, adhering to a belief system, or being obedient to a program.

Freedom to just be... you.

SOBER INTENTIONS

*Sober is making your days count,
not counting the days, you don't drink.*

My wish for you is to explore sober in a whole new way. To be more accurate the true definition and original meaning of the sober.

Sober is making your days count, not counting the days you don't drink.

Sober is being the creator of your life.

Sober is being conscious and in charge of your decisions. *When we are in a distracted state of mind, whether by substance or emotion, we don't always make well informed, intelligent, and thoughtful decisions.*

Sober is being intentional and moving *forward* in life. If you're not growing, you're dying. Choose life.

Sober is being directed by a goal, dream, or aspiration that pulls you forward. Everything is filtered through, "does this move me forward or send me back?"

Sober is realizing you have a finite number of days. Let this light a fire under your butt to consciously make memories and moments that matter.

Let's get started!

No more shutting down
No more silence
No more shame

It's time to wake up and take charge!

*Sober is making your days count,
not counting the days, you don't drink.*

Let's get the basics out of the way. I want you to understand sober is an optimal way to live life, and abstinence is not required to be sober.

And when you get that, a world of options opens in front of you.

I am ever curious and love looking up the definitions and origins of words.

Especially when I get mixed messages, and something doesn't feel right such as what is sober.

When I first stopped drinking going to outpatient and then AA, I cannot tell you how many people I watched struggle constantly thinking about drinking. It's all they talked about.

I didn't understand the struggle. I wanted to get on with my life, and that's where my focus was.

I thought that alcohol had made a mess of my life, and I wasn't going to keep thinking about it when I decided to move forward.

The definition and origin of the word sober explains it well.

DEFINING SOBER

*Sober is making your days count,
not counting the days, you don't drink.*

WEBSTER DICTIONARY

sober
adjective

1a: sparing in the use of food and drink:
ABSTEMIOUS *Moderation*
b: **not addicted to intoxicating drink**
> *Interesting... currently addiction is framed as an incurable brain disease. You will never not be addicted, so you could never BE sober.*

c: not drunk

2: marked by sedate or gravely or earnestly thoughtful character or demeanor

3: UNHURRIED, CALM

4: marked by temperance, moderation, or seriousness a sober candlelight vigil

5: subdued in tone or color

6: showing no excessive or extreme qualities of fancy, emotion, or prejudice
sober
verb
transitive verb: to make sober
intransitive verb: to become sober —usually used with up

The Webster dictionary definition alone supports the position that sober is not abstinence. But let's take it further, to old text, because it's important to understand what it means to be sober.

> *Sober is making your days count,
> not counting the days, you don't drink.*

LATINLEXICON.ORG

The word 'sober' comes from the Latin word "sobrius" and means:

Free from drunkenness

Moderate

Continent

Self-possessed

Prudent

Cautious

SOBER REFERENCES

*Sober is making your days count,
not counting the days, you don't drink.*

True heroism is remarkably sober, very undramatic. It is not the urge to surpass all others at whatever cost, but the urge to serve others at whatever cost. -- Arthur Ashe 1943-1993

Sobriety is the strength of the soul, for it preserves its reason unclouded by passion. Pythagoras ancient Greek philosopher

Sobriety is love of health, or inability to eat much. Francois de la Rochefoucauld 1613-1680

There is nothing wrong with sobriety in moderation. John Ciardi *This might sound like it's referencing alcohol or drinking but it's not. I do find the sarcastic twist humorous though. What it is speaking to is that politeness or humility is what is left over from rich ancestors after the money is gone.*

And this...

"The use of the words' **sober** and temperate **In the use of spirituous liquors**,' In insurance policies, *does not imply that, in order for a man to be sober and temperate, he should abstain from the use of intoxicating liquors*; and the fact that a man may have been drunk on some occasions does not of Itself make him an in temperate man. Wolf v. Mutual Ben. Life Ins. Co. (U. S.) 30 Fed. Cas. 407, 409."

JUDICIAL AND STATUTORY DEFINITIONS OF WORDS AND PHRASES 1905

*Sober is making your days count,
not counting the days, you don't drink.*

FOR THE BIBLE TELLS ME SO

Following are the definitions of sober, according to the King James version of the Bible. Whether you're Christian or not, consider the meaning of the word sober from this ancient text.

Sober was never used in the context of abstinence.

*Sober is making your days count,
not counting the days, you don't drink.*

THE KING JAMES BIBLE

LATIN
SO'BER, a. L. sobrius.

1. Temperate in the use of spirituous liquors; habitually temperate; as a sober man. Live a sober, righteous, and godly life.

2. Not intoxicated or overpowered by spirituous liquors; not drunken. The sot may, at times, be sober.

3. Not mad or insane; not wild, visionary, or heated with passion; having the regular exercise of cool, dispassionate reason. There was not a sober person to be had; all was tempestuous and blustering. Not sober man would put himself in danger, for the applause of escaping without breaking his neck.

4. Regular; calm; not under the influence of passion; as sober judgment; a man in his sober senses.5. Serious; solemn; grave; as the sober livery of autumn.

SOBER ORIGIN
LATIN SOBRIUS

SOBER SCRIPTURE

*Sober is making your days count,
not counting the days, you don't drink.*

---

1 Peter 5:8 AMP Be sober (well balanced and self-disciplined), be alert and cautious at all times. That enemy of yours, the devil, prowls around like a roaring lion [fiercely hungry], seeking someone to devour.

1 Thessalonians 5:6 So then let us not sleep as others do, but let us be alert and sober (be alert and aware)

Romans 12:3 For I say, through the grace given unto me, to every man that is among you, not to think of himself more highly than he ought to think; but to think soberly (soundly, competently), according as God hath dealt to every man the measure of faith.

2 Timothy 4:5 ESV As for you, always be sober-minded (clear headed, steadfast), endure suffering, do the work of an evangelist, fulfill your ministry.

1 Timothy 3:2 ESV Therefore an overseer must be above reproach, the husband of one wife, sober-minded (clear headed, steadfast), self-controlled, respectable, hospitable, able to teach,

Titus 2:2 ESV Older men are to be sober-minded (clear headed, focused), dignified, self-controlled, sound in faith, in love, and in steadfastness.

PINK CLOUD
coaching

Bottom line: Sober and abstinent in the truest sense of the words are not the same.

Somewhere along the line, sober has been misaligned to mean abstinence when in fact, that's not the original and true definition.

Sober is freedom.

*Sober is making your days count,
not counting the days, you don't drink.*

True sobriety provides grace, learning, and growing.

Whereas abstinence is unforgiving, black and white, all or nothing.

Okay, so now what?

Glad you asked.

When we take abstinence off the table, we can explore all the possibilities of being sober.

We don't constantly think I can't drink. And our "sober" success is not measured by drinking or not drinking, but on the value, you're building in life.

I have discovered that this is one of the primary keys to help you break free and live intentionally, creating a life you desire and being the greatest expression of who you were meant to be.

It's a step beyond "sober"--it's what I call living Wholly Sober.

*Sober is making your days count,
not counting the days, you don't drink.*

You are empowered to choose!

I had to feel like I had a choice. In truth, we always have a choice, but when you think you can't drink, it almost makes it more like a dare. How dare you tell me I can't drink even if it's me!

When I allowed myself to be aware that I could drink, but it would screw up my progress and plans, drinking had no pull on me.

Can you see how much more powerful this is?

Traditionally, having a choice is not an option. I think that's where we feel the pressure of all or nothing, and most of us just aren't that confident and CHOOSE to say screw it and drink.

I think there's a little rebel in all of us.

Any thoughts yet?

You can write anything you want.

No one ever has to see it.

*Sober is making your days count,
not counting the days, you don't drink.*

STAGES?

DRUNK
I had been rethinking my drinking for years before I found myself so exhausted and not thinking clearly that I fell victim to a conman. I was vulnerable to his promises and lies. I came to be physically, mentally, and emotionally abused by a man I refer to as Prince Harming in my first book, Wholly Sober.

I call this my drunk stage because I was going through motions just to survive, whether I was drinking or not. In the last year of my drinking, I did remain uncomfortably numb with alcohol.

RECOVERY
Several months into my "sobriety' I faced two business bankruptcies, personal bankruptcy, over fifty thousand in tax debt, an empty bank account, joblessness, homelessness, and rejection by my sponsor and community.

I call this recovery stage because I wasn't clear of mind yet. I was going through what the program was telling me and not thinking for myself. I was managing a disease.

SOBER
Nobody knew me--not the real me. I didn't even know me until I made some really hard and terrifying decisions and took charge of my life, becoming Wholly Sober. I share more about being Wholly Sober later.

*Sober is making your days count,
not counting the days, you don't drink.*

---

*Hint: Being Wholly Sober is simply living by
the true meaning of sober.*

SOBER THOUGHTS

*Sober is making your days count,
not counting the days, you don't drink.*

The first step is simply to get curious.

When you first started drinking, what was it that appealed to you?

What appeals to you now about drinking?

What's changed about how you experience drinking from the beginning until now?

What's drinking getting in the way of?

What's drinking costing you?

I'm not asking you even to consider abstinence. I just want you to get curious and explore your relationship with alcohol.

When we make it okay not to demonize alcohol and instead get curious, we learn a whole lot more.

*Sober is making your days count,
not counting the days, you don't drink.*

SOBER FOCUSED

When your focus is only on drinking or not drinking, you miss the important work--the work that will have your habit of drinking lose its grip.

I want to encourage you to focus on what really matters.

Who do you want to be?

How you want to live?

What you want to do?

How do you want to show up for your loved ones?

Where your focus goes energy flows.

*Sober is making your days count,
not counting the days, you don't drink.*

ALCOHOLISM (SUD) or COPING

Most people I talk with that are trying to change their drinking ways do not identity as alcoholic(s) or having a SUD. They are simply misusing alcohol to numb out, dumb down, or shut off from pain.

Especially pain from memories, should-haves, ought to's, and what-ifs.

They are consumed with thoughts like these:

What if this is as good as it gets...

I should have finished school...

I missed my chance...

I ought to be happy with this life **I designed**...

I just want to get through...

And many times, they don't have immediate access to what they are dissatisfied with, disappointed about, or feel disconnected from.

It's buried under layers of reasoning.

*Sober is making your days count,
not counting the days, you don't drink.*

FOR THE RECORD

SOBER

I'm not a medical professional. I am a trained and certified coach experienced in drinking a lot of booze, getting in a lot of trouble, and making many mistakes that led me to feel helpless, hopeless, and trapped.

I learned, like so many women do, how to cope by misusing alcohol.

I learned how to avoid life pain.

I learned how to push through life and not care about anyone, including myself.

And then, I learned how to do life differently.

I learned I was not born an alcoholic.

I learned that my brain changed with my habit, and it could change again with time, intention, and practice.

I learned that I was not my struggle.

Sometimes we develop a habit of misusing alcohol to just get by and survive.

We medicate with alcohol to tolerate the pain of choices that don't serve us.

*Sober is making your days count,
not counting the days, you don't drink.*

Sober Revolution is not about addiction or substance.

Sober Revolution is about normalizing the desire to want to make the most of life by living awake and aware, making conscious choices, being on purpose and spending our days in purpose, while focusing on what matters most.

It's where we look at sobriety as an empowered choice, a desired way of life, an opportunity to fully express who we are and how we want to leave our mark.

Instead of feeling sentenced for bad behavior, not having a choice, my spouse will leave, I will lose my job, or I can't drink.

NO DIAGNOSIS NECESSARY

*Sober is making your days count,
not counting the days, you don't drink.*

You decide you want to take charge of your relationship with alcohol or _____ (fill in the blank.)

Abstinence is not required to live wholly sober, neither is addiction!

Sober is being awake, aware, and conscious of your choices and actions.

You take full responsibility for your decisions and your life.

The focus is not on drinking or not drinking.

You learn to identify and communicate your needs.

But wait there's more...

You learn to identify and express your feelings in a helpful way.

You learn to identify desires and goals that make you feel fulfilled, inspired, and alive.

You are intentional by creating a plan so you can go after life.

You build trust and confidence through every positive choice and change you make.

You learn from your past, not dwell in it.

You practice your new habit of making conscious choices to *fill up on life,* not booze, drugs, food, social media, tv, or the endless opportunities to dumb down.

*Sober is making your days count,
not counting the days, you don't drink.*

WHOLLY SOBER

Wholly Sober is taking charge and being a constant creator in your life.

Living life deliberately!

Wholly Sober is living with:

Clear Mind

Open Heart

Defined Intention

What does that mean to you?

*Sober is making your days count,
not counting the days, you don't drink.*

Wholly Sober means getting to a place where alcohol (or any other vice) does not have a hold on you, and you *Go-After-Life* with:

A clear mind – you have created strategies and systems to keep your mind clear of overthinking, fogginess, judgment, and negative self-talk. You are awake and calm and able to handle life as it comes. You are not distracted. You are present and aware.

An open heart – you leave space for the what else. You look for love in all things. And peace is your guide. You don't judge your actions or thoughts as good or bad instead, and you observe your choices regarding whether they support your defined intention. Being flexible in your journey.

And defined intention – You have purpose and meaning. You know who you want to be, what you want to do, and how you want to live. You are not walking aimlessly through life. No more survival mode. You do not settle, and you do not live according to what pleases someone else.

Wholly Sober means taking into consideration your whole self. Which may include and are not limited to the following:

	(MIND thoughts and beliefs)
SOURCE SOUL/SPIRIT/SELF	(BODY physical)
	(HEART feelings, emotions)

When we drink or do anything that distracts us from being present and intentional, we become disconnected from SELF.

SELF is who we were born to be.

SELF before the influences, programming both intentional and not, and the expectations of should.

SELF is the voice that many of us can no longer hear without stillness and calm.

SELF who knows the way to our peace.

SELF the direct connect to Source.

If you're disconnected from SELF, how could you be connected to the SOURCE of life, Creator of all things, God?

*Sober is making your days count,
not counting the days, you don't drink.*

If you are walking through life with grudges, shame, guilt, resentment, anger, and not drinking... you are not Wholly Sober.

Wholly Sober is more than not drinking. You may have the occasional glass of wine and be Wholly Sober—If you are not misusing it or getting drunk.

Because you are not opting out of living your life awake and aware, you are not altering your state of being; or compromising your ability to make conscious choices.

When you drink enough to lose your ability to make conscious choices, you are not sober by anyone's definition.

When you do it habitually, it's time to pause and pay attention. That's probably why you are here.

Wholly Sober includes moderate drinking when alcohol is used to celebrate an event or enhance a moment. But never to numb out, dumb down, avoid or forget.

Alcohol should never be used to check out of your life.

Keep in mind that this is your one and only precious life. Anytime that you are drunk or buzzed, it is life you choose NOT TO LIVE during that time. It's forfeited. Your choice!

You have an opportunity to root into a resolve to moderate or abstain by living Wholly Sober.

Journaling can help you create great awareness and offer you new insight. If you're interested, I've created 28 Day Journal – Explore, available on Amazon.

Your mind will become clear, and you will be able to define your intention to move forward in your journey with an open heart. The possibilities are limitless.

Wholly Sober is not about whether you drink or not.

It's about whether you are LIVING your life or going through the motions until you have no life left to live and misusing alcohol to ignore that truth.

*Sober is making your days count,
not counting the days, you don't drink.*

SOBER POSSIBILITIES

A healthy loving marriage.

Being able to make bold, confident career decisions.

Setting firm boundaries to keep your peace.

Using peace as your guide to make changes.

Knowing what matters to you and standing up for it.

Being strong, confident, and bold.

Being and having loyal, trusting, and fun friendships.

The courage and confidence to step out of your comfort zone.

Free to be who you choose to be.

Sober is Freedom

> *Sober is making your days count,*
> *not counting the days, you don't drink.*

These are just some of the possibilities of a Wholly Sober life.

What would you add?

What are the possibilities of BEING sober for YOU?

How do you want to live the rest of your life?

WHAT'S RIGHT FOR YOU

*Sober is making your days count,
not counting the days, you don't drink.*

Only you can decide.

Maybe take a moment and write down your thoughts.

Here are a few questions for you to consider.

Are you endangering yourself or others?

For instance, are you driving and not remembering how you got home, or is it a great big blur?

Are you able to make conscious choices to drink or not drink?

For instance, you have a business trip where you can't drink. Are you okay?

These questions are not a self-diagnosis test.

These are simple questions to help you think about your drinking.

COLLABORATION

*Sober is making your days count,
not counting the days, you don't drink.*

Does Sober Revolution resonate with you?

Are you ready to take charge of your drinking, your LIFE?

Do you want to create and live life inspired and intentional?

Do you have an audience that needs to hear and would benefit from this message?

Do you have a complementary business or job and would like to chat about a possible collaboration?

Do you have a story of finding sober freedom without the ISMS of traditional recovery?

Let's talk!

PinkCloudCoaching.com

Together we can normalize being sober by making sober a desired way to live for *all people* and end the stigma that hinders so many from reaching out for support.

*Sober is making your days count,
not counting the days, you don't drink.*

PINK CLOUD COACHING
It's not your ordinary run of the mill approach to sobriety...
it gives you LIFE!

THREE AREAS OF FOCUS

*Sober is making your days count,
not counting the days, you don't drink.*

PAIN

Today I help women change their drinking habit by shifting their focus from alcohol to what really matters to them. I help them explore with gentle curiosity where their "pain" lies.

By pain, I mean emotions not being expressed or understood, dreams being tucked away, conversations not being had, truth not being spoken typically, out of fear of disrupting everything that is "okay."

Is okay, okay?

CONNECTION

I help them remember who they are and reconnect to SELF instead of existing uncomfortably numb, checking off the should and supposed to's.

Together we create strategies and collect tools to support them in THEIR specific needs, desires, and challenges.

What I have found to be true is the problem is rarely about the alcohol.

*Sober is making your days count,
not counting the days, you don't drink.*

BECOMING

One of the major contributors to my sober success is focusing on the future I wanted.

I can still remember the feeling in my body and the hope in my heart, visualizing who I could be without canceling out my potential with alcohol.

I remember thinking, what could I do with what I know now?

In Wholly Sober, I called it "daydreaming and doing."

Never forget, you are not who you were, and you are not done!

Take a minute now and ask yourself...

Who do I want to become?

RESOURCES

SCHEDULE A FREE CONSULTATION:
If you'd like to explore working together, let's chat! Just visit pinkcloudcoaching.com and click on the bright pink bar that says "Schedule Appointment"
https://www.pinkcloudcoaching.com/appointment-booking/

GET CENTERED:
The quick breathing exercise to ground you
https://www.pinkcloudcoaching.com/grounding-meditation/

ORDER WHOLLY SOBER:
https://www.WhollySoberBook.com

ORDER THE PRIMED DRINKER:
https://www.PrimedDrinker.com

ORDER EXPLORE: 28 DAY JOURNAL:
https://www.amazon.com/dp/1678509914

YOUTUBE:
Teresa Rodden Pink Cloud Coaching

FACEBOOK:
Teresa Rodden Pink Cloud Coaching

INSTAGRAM:
PINK CLOUD COACHING

SIGN UP FOR EVENTS/PROGRAMS/UPDATES
Pink Cloud Coaching

*Sober is making your days count,
not counting the days, you don't drink.*

ABOUT THE AUTHOR

Teresa Rodden is a certified personal coach, speaker, and founder of Pink Cloud Coaching, established in 2012. She advocates for a Sober Revolution, normalizing sober by empowering people with tips, tools, and truth where addiction and abstinence are not required. Making sober the desired state of being for all people is how we end the stigma.

She delights in accompanying women on soulful journeys to discover THEIR sober path by reconnecting to self and finding divine inspiration through the Pink Cloud process.

PinkCloudCoaching.com

Printed in Great Britain
by Amazon